Mix-n-Match Recipes

Creative Ideas for Today's Busy Kitchens

DEBORAH TAYLOR-HOUGH

DEDICATION

For Kelsey. Hope you can find some ideas for meals here.
After all, Substitutions-R-Us.

CONTENTS

ACKNOWLEDGMENTS

Thank you to Brook at Champion Press for publishing the 2nd Edition of this small book and then seeing that it continued on by moving it to SourceBooks (3rd Edition). And now it's back where it all began—at Simple Pleasures Press. Welcome home, little Mix-n-Match Recipes (4th Edition)!

INTRODUCING
MIX-N-MATCH RECIPES

"What's for dinner, Mom?" Have you ever heard that question in your house? I think I heard it nearly every day of the week and at least half a dozen times on weekends for 20+ years. It'd be nice to have an easy answer to that question each night. But, honestly, sometimes the cupboard's bare and time is severely limited. It's hard to answer that dinner question then.

Ever been there? I know I have. Even one of those crazy busy days with hungry kids, empty shelves, or no time, can add up to another quick call to the pizza delivery guy. If you add tight finances into the equation, it's pretty much impossible to order fast food, or even run out to the store for last-minute ingredients to prepare a new recipe from your favorite magazine, website, or idea board.

On those "Old Mother Hubbard days" when the troops are clamoring for something more nourishing than dry ramen noodles straight from the package, wouldn't it be great to transform that lonely can of stewed tomatoes, a stray packet of chicken soup mix, a few partially emptied pasta boxes, and some frozen mixed vegetables into something tasty for the family?

Well, welcome to my world—the world of Mix-n-Match Recipes. Making a real meal out of assorted odds and ends from the pantry and refrigerator? Is it possible? Is it even edible? You bet it is! If I had to pick a personal motto, it would be "Happiness is making the most of what you have." Not only is it a good motto to live by, it's also an accurate description of the philosophy behind this book's collection of recipes. The concept of Mix-n-Match Recipes is making the most of what you have in your pantry, refrigerator, and freezer.

No more last minute trips to the store. No more panic about what to eat when you run out of money before you run out of month. As long as you can unearth a few dusty cans on a shelf somewhere, there's a good chance a Mix-n-Match meal awaits. These recipe ideas cover the entire gamut of eating … soups, appetizers, desserts, main meals, snacks. If you can name it, you can probably Mix-n-Match it!

The recipes in this book are the result of creatively meeting the needs and desires of my family over many years of living on a tight budget with competing demands on my time and energy. Sounds a bit like the story of modern American life, doesn't it? Extremely busy, sometimes broke, but always resilient and resourceful.

Not all of the experiments on our family's way to Mix-n-Match heaven were a success—but just the process itself was always a lot of fun. Even my three kids learned to enjoy making their own Mix-n-Match soups and skillet meals when it was their turn to cook for the family. Never knowing how the final product would turn out was half the fun—a true adventure in eating.

Do you remember that old children's story, Stone Soup? Everyone came along and threw a little of this and a little of that into the pot with the stone, and before their eyes—and ta da!—the first unofficial Mix-and-Match soup was born! And remember how much they all loved it? I've learned that contributing something to the finished product goes a long way toward increasing a child's enjoyment of their meal.

Just think of Mix-n-Match cooking as an art form all its own. I'll give you the general guidelines and starting points—you take it from there and see what tasty concoctions your kitchen has hiding in the dark recesses of its shelves and drawers. To get started using this book, you won't need to run out to the store to stock up on hard to find ingredients. Just pick from what you already have on hand. I wish you many years of happy cooking in your busy—and creative—kitchen.

Deborah Taylor-Hough
Seattle/Tacoma 2015

MIX-N-MATCH SOUP

The other day, I spent so much time working on my latest decluttering project, I completely forgot to even think about what we're going to have for dinner that night. Oops. Sadly, this isn't exactly a rare occurrence in my house. But I have a back-up plan for those nights when I forget to think about dinner. Basically I can clear out my cupboards and fridge and make a delicious homemade soup. Mix-n-Match Soup, you're my hero!

This is a seriously simple way to make a meal out of whatever's hiding in the back recesses of your cupboards or freezer. It's the answer to the age old question, "What do we eat when there's nothing to eat?" It's like the classic children's story, Stone Soup. Only in this version, we make it without the stone! Although I suppose that's always an option. But, um, no. I think we'd better not use an actual stone. I'd probably break a tooth.

Mix-and-Match Soup
(8 generous servings)

Broth (choose one)

1. **Tomato:** One 12-ounce can of tomato paste plus two 16-ounce cans of tomatoes with juice (chopped) plus water to equal 10 cups total
2. **Chicken/Turkey:** 10 cups broth or 4 bouillon cubes dissolved in 10 cups of water
3. **Beef:** 10 cups broth or 4 bouillon cubes dissolved in 10 cups of water

Protein (choose one — 1 pound or 2 cups, cooked)

- Ground beef, browned
- Leftover meatballs or meatloaf, chopped
- Cooked chicken or turkey (cut up)
- Ham (cut up)
- Lentils
- Frankfurters, sliced (or any sausage or Kielbasa)
- Pepperoni, sliced
- Beans, cooked or canned (pintos, kidney, Great Northern, etc.)

Grain (choose 1 or 2 for a total of 2 cups)

- Rice, cooked (any variety)
- Barley, cooked
- Pasta, raw
- Corn
- Dumplings (add near end of cooking time)

Vegetables (raw, cooked or canned, choose 2 or more for a total of 1 to 2 cups)

- Cabbage
- Carrots
- Celery
- Onion
- Potatoes
- Tomatoes
- Green beans
- Turnips
- Parsnips
- Broccoli
- Peas or pea pods

- Cauliflower
- Bell pepper
- Zucchini (add raw)

Seasonings (choose 2 to 4 spices, 1 to 2 teaspoons each)

- Basil
- Cayenne (dash)
- Chives
- Cumin
- Garlic
- Marjoram
- Onion powder
- Thyme
- Rosemary
- Parsley
- Oregano
- Spice mix

Preparation:

1. Bring the broth to a boil in a large stockpot or Dutch oven.
2. Add all of the ingredients; salt and pepper to taste.
3. Reduce heat and simmer one hour.

Slow Cooker Prep:

- Pour boiling stock and other ingredients into a slow cooker and simmer for 8 to 12 hours or overnight on LOW setting.

MIX-N-MATCH QUICHE

You can use almost any leftover vegetable or meat in this recipe. If you have eggs, milk, rice, and cheese, you can practically clean out your fridge right into your quiche pan. I always add the cheese last when making this quiche. The cheese makes a beautiful mellow-brown crust on the top. I usually add a bit of chopped onion to my quiches for flavor, and broccoli makes an especially nice vegetable quiche.

Mix-n-Match Quiche
(6 servings)

Crust Ingredients:

- 2 cups rice, cooked (white or brown)
- 1 egg, beaten
- 1 tsp soy sauce*

Filling Ingredients:

- ½ lb. any leftover vegetable, chopped (single vegetable or a mix)
- 4 eggs, beaten
- 1½ cups milk, or light cream
- 1 cup cheese, grated (your choice: Swiss, Cheddar, Jack, etc.)
- ½ tsp salt (optional)
- ¼ tsp pepper
- Dash nutmeg, or ground mace

Crust Directions:

1. Mix together cooked rice, egg, and soy sauce.
2. Spread evenly to cover well-buttered quiche pan or pie plate.
3. Bake rice crust at 350 F for 10 minutes.
4. Remove from oven.

Filling Directions:

1. Place chopped vegetable in bottom of crust.
2. Mix together: eggs, milk, salt, pepper and nutmeg. Pour over vegetable.
3. Top with grated cheese. Bake at 350 F for 45 minutes, or until set.
4. Remove from oven, and let sit ten minutes before slicing, if serving fresh; or wrap pie pan, label and freeze.
5. Quiche can be served cold after thawing for a yummy hot weather treat or lunch item; or heat the thawed quiche at 350 F for 20 minutes.

---

*Gluten-Free Suggestion:

To make this gluten-free, leave out the soy sauce or use a gluten-free brand.

CREAM-OF-WHATEVER SOUP SUBSTITUTE

Use this recipe in place of any canned cream soups you may find in recipes. You can freeze the prepared sauce in a plastic container with tight-fitting lid, allowing enough head space for expansion. Can be frozen for up to 3 months. Defrost in the refrigerator overnight. Reheat thoroughly and stir to recombine before serving.

Cream-of-Whatever Soup Substitute
(equal to 1 can of cream-of-whatever soup)

Basic Sauce (thick):

- 3 Tablespoons butter or oil
- 3 Tablespoons flour
- ¼ teaspoon salt
- dash of pepper
- 1¼ cup liquid, milk or stock

Directions:

1. Melt butter or oil in saucepan.
2. Stir in flour and seasonings.
3. Cook over medium heat until bubbly.
4. Add liquid slowly, stirring with wire whisk to prevent lumps.
5. Cook until thick.
6. Makes 1 cup or 1 can of condensed soup.

Easy Varieties:

- **Cream of Tomato:** Use tomato juice for the liquid. Add dashes of garlic, onion powder, basil, and oregano.
- **Cream of Chicken:** Use chicken broth for half the liquid. Add ¼ teaspoon poultry seasoning or sage.
- **Cream of Mushroom** (or celery or chive): Sauté ¼ cup chopped mushrooms, celery or chives and 1 tablespoon minced onion in butter before adding flour.

Allergy Suggestion:

If you use a gluten-free flour (rice, tapioca, etc.) or cornstarch, you can make this soup gluten-free. And if you use stock rather than milk, and use oil rather than butter, you can make it dairy-free, too.

MIX-N-MATCH SKILLET MEALS

The following recipe is one I prepare regularly to use up leftovers or clear out the cupboards. I keep a copy of this taped to the inside of my pantry door at all times. I'm always amazed at the meals I can create from these simple, basic formulas. I also save money by choosing ingredients I have on hand. Sometimes I even surprise myself with a delicious nearly-gourmet combination or two! Also an excellent way to use up leftover turkey or ham from your holiday dinners.

Mix-n-Match Skillet Meals
(4 to 6 servings)

Choose 1 food from each of the following groups:

Breads and Cereals (1 cup raw)

- Macaroni
- Spaghetti
- Rice, cooked or raw (white or brown)
- Noodles
- Bulgar
- Any pasta

Sauce (1 can soup plus $1\frac{1}{2}$ cans milk, broth or water)

- Cream of Mushroom
- Cream of Celery
- Cream of Chicken
- Cream of Potato

- Tomato Soup
- French Onion Soup
- Cream-of-Whatever Soup Substitute (from page 8)

Protein (1 pound or 1 cup cooked)

- Chopped beef
- Chopped pork or ham
- Ground beef or turkey
- Chicken
- Turkey
- Tuna
- Salmon
- Mackerel
- Cooked dry beans
- Frankfurters
- Keilbasa

Vegetables (1½ to 2 cups canned, cooked or raw)

- Carrots
- Peas
- Corn
- Green beans
- Lima beans
- Broccoli
- Spinach
- Mixed vegetables
- Celery
- Green Pepper
- Whatever you have around

½ to 1 cup cheese (any kind) can be stirred into sauce at the end of the cooking time.

Instructions:

1. Choose one food from each of the four groups above.
2. Stir together in skillet.
3. Season to taste with salt, pepper, soy sauce, onion flakes, garlic, or whatever spices you enjoy.
4. Bring to a boil.
5. Reduce heat to lowest setting.
6. Cover pan and simmer 30 minutes until pasta or rice is tender.
7. Stir occasionally to prevent rice or pasta from sticking.
8. Stir in cheese, if desired.
9. Serve.
10. Makes 4 to 6 servings.

To bake in oven: Mix all ingredients in casserole dish and cover tightly; bake at 350 F for 1 hour.

PASTA PRESTO

This is a recipe given to me many years ago by a long-time friend. I personally don't use this one often, but she says she couldn't live without it. That's how I feel about the Mix-n-Match Soup recipe, so your mileage may vary between these assorted recipe ideas.

Pasta Presto
(4 servings)

Choose 8-ounces of one of the following:

- Vermicelli
- Fettuccini
- Angel Hair Pasta
- Spaghetti
- Egg Noodles

Choose one of the following:

- 6 slices turkey bacon, cut into 1-inch pieces
- ¾ cup ham, cubed
- ½ pound ground beef, turkey, or pork
- ½ pound chicken breasts, cut into pieces

Choose one of the following:

- 1 cup frozen peas
- 1 cup broccoli florets
- 1 cup French-style green beans

Choose one of the following:

- 1 jar prepared Alfredo sauce
- 1 jar prepared marinara or spaghetti sauce

You may also wish to add 6 green onions, sliced thinly.

Directions:

1. Cook pasta as directed on box and drain.
2. While pasta is cooking, cook your meat of choice until crisp or browned.
3. Stir in one jar of sauce.
4. Stir in cooked noodles and vegetables.
5. Cook for another ten minutes or until heated through and vegetables are crisp-tender.

CREATE-A-CASSEROLE

This is another recipe from the same friend who gave me the Pasta Presto recipe. I usually just use the oven version of the Mix-n-Match Skillet Meals recipe when I want a casserole.

Create-a-Casserole
(6 servings)

Choose one food from each of the following categories unless otherwise noted

Protein – 1 lbs. or 1½ cups cooked

- Tuna (1 can)
- Ground beef, pork or turkey
- Ham, cut up
- Eggs, hard cooked and chopped
- Chopped beef, pork or ham
- Chicken or turkey cut up
- Fish, cooked and cut up
- Frankfurters, sausage or Kielbasa (cooked and cut up)

Vegetables – 1½ to 2 cups canned, cooked or raw

- Green beans
- Peas
- Spinach
- Mixed vegetables
- Corn
- Other vegetable of your choosing

Grains – 1 cup raw

- Spaghetti
- Macaroni
- Potatoes, sliced and cubed
- Pasta (any)
- Rice (white or brown)
- Bulgar
- Millet
- Quick cook barley

Sauce – 1 can plus 1½ same-size-soup cans of milk or water, or 2 cups sauce of your choice

- Cream of Potato, Chicken, Celery, Asparagus, or Mushroom soup
- Cream-of-Whatever Soup Substitute (from this book)
- Tomato soup
- French onion soup
- White sauce (homemade)
- Sour cream
- Stewed tomatoes, undrained plus 1 can water or broth

Extras – choose 1 or 2, up to 1 cup total

- Pimento
- Almonds, sliced or slivered

Topping – 1 cup

- Potato chips or round buttery crackers, crushed
- Cheese, grated
- Stuffing mix or bread crumbs
- Parmesan cheese

Directions:

1. Choose one food from each of the groups above.
2. Thoroughly mix together (except for topping).
3. Season to taste with salt, pepper, soy sauce, onion flakes, garlic or whatever spices you enjoy using in casseroles.
4. Place in buttered casserole dish; sprinkle on choice of topping.
5. Bake uncovered at 350 F for 1 hour.

MIX-N-MATCH FRIED RICE

If you make a lot of rice like I do, I recommend you think about buying a rice cooker. I did without one for many years, but since receiving one for a gift several Christmases ago, I can't imagine being without one ever again! Even with only two of us at home now, I still use it several times each week.

Mix-and-Match Fried Rice
(6 servings)

Ingredients:

- 12-ounces regular long grain white rice
- 1½ tablespoons plus 2 teaspoons sesame oil
- 1½ cup onion, finely chopped
- 2 teaspoons fresh ginger root, pared and minced (or ½ teaspoon dried)
- 3 teaspoons minced garlic
- 1 teaspoon red pepper flakes
- 2 eggs, beaten
- 5 tablespoons soy sauce (or tamari)

Veggies – choose 2 or 3

- 1 medium zucchini, cut into ½ inch pieces
- 1 bell pepper (red, yellow, or green) coarsely chopped
- 1 cup snow peas, stem ends and veins removed, cut into 1 inch pieces
- 9 asparagus spears, cut into ½ inch pieces
- 1 cup broccoli, cut into small pieces

- 4 green onion, sliced
- 1 cup leeks, cut into thin strips
- 1 cup carrots, thinly sliced or diced
- 2 celery ribs, sliced thinly

Protein – choose 1

- 2 cups cooked chicken or turkey, cut into ½-inch pieces
- 2 cups cooked shrimp (can used canned)
- 2 cups cooked ham, diced
- 1 pound tofu, drained and cut into ½-inch pieces

Directions:

1. Cook rice according to package directions.
2. In large skillet or wok, sauté onion, ginger, garlic, and pepper flakes in 1½ tablespoons sesame oil.
3. Cook over medium-high heat for two minutes.
4. Add your choice of Mix-n-Match vegetables.
5. Cook, stirring frequently, 3 to 4 minutes, until vegetables are just starting to soften.
6. Stir in your choice of Mix-n-Match cooked meat and continue cooking until heated through.
7. In a separate pan, scramble eggs.
8. Gently stir eggs and vegetable mixture into rice.
9. Stir in soy sauce.
10. Saute in skillet for five minutes more with 2 teaspoons sesame oil, stirring frequently.
11. Serve hot.

MIX-N-MATCH RICE BOWLS

Rice bowls are an easy, inexpensive and delicious way to combine leftover rice with other healthy foods such as vegetables and lean proteins.

Mix-n-Match Rice Bowls
(1 serving)

- 1 cup of cooked rice
- 1 cup vegetables
- 2-3 ounces of protein (meat, beans, tofu)
- ½ cup shredded cheese (optional)
- Your choice of seasonings

Layer ingredients in bowl. Add sauce or seasonings of your choice. Especially good with Mexican-style seasonings and topped with sour cream, salsa, and sliced black olives.

RICE "STIR-IN" IDEAS

To 1 cup of cooked rice (your choice of white, brown, basmati, long-grain, etc.), stir-in any of the following combinations for a tasty lunch, easy dinner, or simple side dish.

Mix-n-Match Rice "Stir-In" Ideas

1. Dried cranberries, chopped pecans, and sliced green onions
2. Thawed frozen peas and chopped ham
3. Chopped chicken, sliced almonds, sliced green onions, and orange marmalade
4. Scrambled eggs, chopped Canadian bacon, and chopped chives
5. Orange segments, sliced almonds, and sliced green onions
6. Granola, vanilla yogurt, and golden raisins
7. Butter, lemon zest, and fresh lemon juice
8. Minced garlic and mushrooms sautéed in butter
9. Diced tomatoes, sliced green onions, and shredded Monterey Jack cheese
10. Scrambled eggs, crumbled sausage, cream cheese cubes, and sliced green onions
11. Zucchini and carrot "matchsticks" sautéed in butter, and Parmesan cheese
12. Thawed frozen corn, mild green chiles, and sour cream

MIX-N-MATCH MUFFIN MEAL

These make a super simple lunch or snack.

Mix-n-Match Muffin Meal
(makes 1 dozen)

Choose one protein and one vegetable:

Protein – 1 cup cooked

- Tuna (1 can)
- Ground beef, pork, or turkey
- Ham, finely cubed or grated
- Chopped beef, pork, or ham
- Chicken
- Turkey
- Fish
- Frankfurters

Vegetable – ½ cup cooked

- Carrots
- Green beans
- Onion
- Corn
- Peas
- Broccoli
- Spinach
- Mixed vegetables

Other Ingredients:

- 1 package refrigerator biscuits
- 2 eggs, lightly beaten
- Shredded cheese for garnish, optional

Preparation:

1. Open the biscuits and separate them.
2. Roll or press each biscuit into a 4 inch wide circle.
3. Place into ungreased muffin tins, spreading across bottom and up the sides of each muffin well to form a small cup (it doesn't have to fill the entire muffin—they will expand as they cook).
4. In a mixing bowl, stir together eggs, meat, and vegetables.
5. Spoon 1 heaping tablespoon of filling into each biscuit cup, top with small amount of cheese (if used).
6. Bake at 350 F until filling is set (about 15-18 minutes).
7. Serve hot.

These can also be served cool from the refrigerator as an easy snack. These can be frozen after preparation and reheated in the microwave.

MIX-N-MATCH QUICK BREAD

I'm always on the lookout for recipes that are quick, easy, family-friendly, inexpensive and flexible. This quick bread meets all of my criteria for a budget-worthy recipe. Plus it's tasty and super-simple, too!

Quick Bread Tips: When making any quick bread (banana bread, zucchini bread, cornbread, etc.) be careful not to overmix. Stir mixture until just combined or it may become heavy and too dense. Also, be sure to bake in the center of the oven where the temperature is the most consistent.

Mix-n-Match Quick Bread
(Makes two loaves)

You can also make 12 muffins with this recipe.

Ingredients:

- 3 cups flour
- 1 teaspoon salt
- 1 tablespoon cinnamon
- ½ teaspoon baking powder
- 1 teaspoon baking soda
- 2 eggs
- 1 cup oil
- 2 cups sugar
- 2 cups Mix-n-Match (see below)
- 1 tablespoon vanilla extract
- 1 cup chopped nuts or seeds, optional (your choice)

Mix-n-Match (one or more of the following to equal 2 cups)

- Apples, grated or chopped
- Applesauce (reduce oil to ½ cup)
- Apricots, chopped
- Bananas, mashed or chopped
- Berries
- Carrots, cooked and mashed or grated
- Cherries, pitted and chopped
- Coconut, grated
- Cranberries, dry or raw, chopped
- Dates or figs, pitted and finely chopped
- Lemon, ½ cup juice
- Marmalade (omit 1 cup sugar)
- Oranges, chopped
- Orange juice, ½ cup juice
- Peaches, fresh or canned, chopped
- Pears, fresh or canned, chopped
- Pineapple, crushed and well-drained
- Prunes, chopped
- Pumpkin, canned
- Raisins
- Rhubarb, finely chopped (add ½ cup more sugar)
- Strawberries, well-drained
- Sweet potatoes or yams, cooked and mashed, or grated
- Zucchini, grated and well-drained

Directions:

1. Sift together dry ingredients.
2. In separate bowl, beat eggs; add oil and sugar; cream together.
3. Stir in vanilla and your choice of Mix-n-Match.

4. Add dry ingredients; mix well.
5. Stir in nuts, if used.
6. Spoon into 2 well-greased loaf pans.
7. Bake at 325 F for 1 hour.

For Muffins:

1. Spoon batter into muffin tins (about half full).
2. Bake at 375 F for 15 minutes.

A sample of tasty Mix-n-Match Quick Bread combinations:

- Carrot-Raisin-Walnut
- Pumpkin-Raisin-Sunflower seeds
- Apple-Cranberry-Walnut
- Cranberry-Orange-Walnut

MIX-N-MATCH FRUIT GRUNT

If you make this recipe with well-drained pineapple chunks or tidbits, it turns out quite a bit like Pineapple Upside-Down Cake.

Mix-and-Match Fruit Grunt
(makes 1 loaf)

Ingredients:

- Any fresh fruit (sliced or cubed—or well-drained canned fruit)
- Any flavor Jiffy™-boxed cake mix
- ½ cup sugar

Directions:

1. Generously butter a bread loaf pan.
2. Place fruit in bottom of pan.
3. Sprinkle with sugar.
4. Prepare cake mix as directed and then pour over fruit in bread pan.
5. Bake as directed on box.
6. Let cool and then invert on a plat to unmold.
7. Serve warm with whipped cream.

MIX-N-MATCH FRUIT CRISP

The first time I ever made this, I was surprised by how easy and delicious it was. I kept feeling like I was doing something wrong by not doing anything with the cake mix except sprinkle it out dry onto the filling. But yes, it's really that easy.

Mix-and-Match Fruit Crisp
(makes 6 servings)

Ingredients:

- 2 cans pie filling (your choice)
- 1 can crushed pineapple
- 1 cup pecans or walnuts (chopped)
- 1 box yellow cake mix
- 1 stick butter or margarine, melted

Preparation:

1. Mix together pie filling and pineapple.
2. Pour into 13-by-9-inch baking pan. Sprinkle with nuts.
3. Dump the dry cake mix directly out of the box onto the filling and nuts mixture. Press lightly to make a smooth top over the filling.
4. Evenly pour melted butter over top of cake mix (spread gently to cover).
5. Bake at 350 F for 30-40 minutes or until the cake top is golden brown (may still be a bit soft at this point, but will form more of a traditional crust as it cools).
6. Cool for 10 minutes. Serve warm or cold.
7. Top with ice cream or whipped cream, if desired.

MIX-N-MATCH YOGURT POPS

Ingredients:

- 2 cups plain (or vanilla) yogurt
- 1 cup milk
- 1 cups mashed fruit (your choice)
- ½ teaspoon vanilla extract

Directions:

1. Mix together yogurt, milk, fruit (your choice), and vanilla extract.
2. Blend by hand until smooth.
3. Pour into freezer pop molds.
4. Freeze.

Or simply mix fruit-flavored yogurt with milk, stir together, then freeze.

EASY PEASY FREEZER POPS

Fudge Pops:

Prepare instant chocolate pudding according to package directions. Pour into freezer pop molds. Freeze until solid.

Rocky Road Pops:

Prepare instant chocolate pudding according to package directions. Stir in ½ cup miniature marshmallows, ¼ cup semisweet chocolate chips, and ¼ cup chopped nuts. Pour into freezer pop molds. Freeze.

Butterscotch Pops:

Prepare instant butterscotch pudding according to package directions, substituting root beer for milk in recipe if desired. Pour into freezer pop molds. Freeze.

Toffee Pops:

Prepare instant vanilla pudding according to package directions. Stir in ½ chopped chocolate covered toffee bars. Pour into freezer pop molds. Freeze.

Fruity Pops:

Stir one cup boiling water into 1 (4-serving size) package of gelatin dessert and ¼ cup sugar. Stir until dissolved. Stir in 1½ cups cold water and mix in your choice of crushed or finely chopped fruit. Pour into freezer pop molds. Freeze.

DRIP-LESS FRUITY FREEZER POPS

Freezer pops made with gelatin desserts don't drip nearly as much as pops made from drink mixes or other liquids.

- **Strawberry**: Use strawberry gelatin with 1 cup pureed strawberries
- **Lemonade**: Use lemon gelatin and ¼ cup fresh lemon juice
- **Watermelon**: Use watermelon gelatin and 1 cup pureed watermelon (seeds removed)
- **Orange Cream**: Use orange gelation and 1 cup evaporated milk in place of water

Use your imagination!

ABOUT THE AUTHOR

Deborah Taylor-Hough is the author of several books including: *Frugal Living For Dummies*®, the best-selling *Frozen Assets* cookbook series, and *A Simple Choice: A practical guide for saving your time, money and sanity.*

Deborah is a graduate of the University of Washington, and is currently in Graduate School pursuing a Master of Fine Arts (MFA) in Creative Writing. She has worked as the Outreach Director and Youth Director at her church, and teaches workshops and seminars throughout the USA and Canada.

Her workshop topics include:

- living within your means
- simple living
- cooking for the freezer
- general homemaking
- writing, publishing and publicity
- identifying personal priorities
- simplifying the holidays
- common sense home education
- ... and more!

Visit Deborah online: TheSimpleMom.com

Also available from Deborah Taylor-Hough

Frozen Assets: Cook for a Day, Eat for a Month
ISBN: 9781402218590 (Sourcebooks)

This breakthrough cookbook delivers a program for readers to cook a week or month's worth of meals in just one day by using easy and affordable recipes to create a customized meal plan. The author, who saved $24,000 on her family's total grocery bill during a five-year period, offers up kid-tested and family-approved recipes in *Frozen Assets*, plus bulk-cooking tips for singles, shopping lists, recipes for two-week and 30-day meal plans, and a ten-day plan to eliminate cooking over the holidays. Cooking for the freezer allows you to plan ahead, purchase items in bulk, cut down on waste, and stop those all-too-frequent trips to the drive-thru.

Frozen Assets Lite and Easy
ISBN: 9781402218606 (Sourcebooks)

Taylor-Hough is back with a book of low-fat, lower-calorie meal plans that use the same time-saving and cost-effective methods. *Frozen Assets Lite and Easy* shows readers how to be healthy while still saving time and money, with shopping lists, recipes, and detailed instruction on how to make freezer cooking work for you.

Frugal Living For Dummies®

ISBN: 9780764554032 (Wiley)

Need help keeping that New Year's resolution to eliminate credit card debt and live within your means? Packed with tips on cutting costs on everything from groceries to gifts for all occasions, this practical guide shows you how to spend less on the things you need and save more for those fun things you want.

A Simple Choice: A practical guide for saving your time, money and sanity

Coming in mid-2015 from Simple Pleasures Press

The number one complaint of people today is the lack of meaning in their hectic lives. In this book, the author addresses societal emptiness and the personal search for contentment. *A Simple Choice* not only examines the futility of keeping up with the Jones', but depicts the simple joy and fulfillment of keeping up with ourselves. Through practical help in the areas of homemaking, family unity, saving money, simple spending plans, easy and frugal cooking, and much more, Taylor-Hough guides us down a simpler life path. In an era of self-reflection, *A Simple Choice* holds the answers to life's simple joys, available to everyone.

To order these and other titles go to:
TheSimpleMom.com

Made in the USA
Monee, IL
01 December 2019